EXPLORING SCIENCE

# MINERALS

## FROM APATITE TO ZINC

### BY DARLENE R. STILLE

Content Adviser: Jim Walker, Professor of Geology and
Environmental Geosciences, Northern Illinois University

Science Adviser: Terrence E. Young Jr., M.Ed., M.L.S.,
Jefferson Parish (Louisiana) Public School System

Reading Adviser: Susan Kesselring, M.A., Literacy Educator,
Rosemount-Apple Valley-Eagan (Minnesota) School District

S

COMPASS POINT BOOKS · MINNEAPOLIS, MINNESOTA

552
STI

Compass Point Books • 3109 West 50th Street, #115 • Minneapolis, MN  55410

Visit Compass Point Books on the Internet at *www.compasspointbooks.com*
or e-mail your request to *custserv@compasspointbooks.com*

Photographs ©: Corbis, cover; J & L Weber/Peter Arnold, Inc., 4, 8, 16 (right); Tom & Therisa Stack/Tom Stack & Associates, 5, 38 (right); Historical Picture Archive/Corbis, 6; Paul A. Souders/Corbis, 7; NASA, 11; Reuters/Corbis, 13; Roger Ressmeyer/Corbis, 15; John Cancalosi/Peter Arnold, Inc., 16 (left); Corel, 17 (left); Kelvin Aitken/Peter Arnold, Inc., 17 (right); Mark A. Schneider/Visuals Unlimited, 19, 23 (right); Wally Eberhart/Visuals Unlimited, 20; Sylvester Alred/Unicorn Stock Photos, 21; Ken Lucas/Visuals Unlimited, 23 (left); BBC Microimaging/Visuals Unlimited, 25; Doug Sokell/Visuals Unlimited, 26; Leonard Lessin/Peter Arnold, Inc., 27; Owen Franken/Corbis, 29; Marli Miller/Visuals Unlimited, 30; Mark E. Gibson/The Image Finders, 31; Brian Parker/Tom Stack & Associates, 32; S.J. Krasemann/Peter Arnold, Inc., 33; Fritz Polking/Peter Arnold, Inc., 34; Allen B. Smith/Tom Stack & Associates, 35; Stuart Jennings, 36; Barnabas Bosshart/Corbis, 37; Steve Kaufman/Peter Arnold, Inc., 38 (left); Kean Collection/Getty Images, 41; Jim Baron/The Image Finders, 42; Howard Davies/Corbis, 43; RITGER-UNEP/Peter Arnold, Inc., 44; Buddy Mays/Corbis, 46.

Art Director: Keith Griffin
Managing Editor: Catherine Neitge
Editor: Nadia Higgins
Photo Researcher: Marcie C. Spence
Designer/Page production: The Design Lab
Lead Designer: Jaime Martins
Illustrator: Farhana Hossain
Educational Consultant: Diane Smolinski

**Library of Congress Cataloging-in-Publication Data**
Stille, Darlene R.
  Minerals : from apatite to zinc / by Darlene R. Stille.
     p. cm. — (Exploring science)
  Includes bibliographical references and index.
  ISBN 0-7565-0855-X (hardcover)
  1. Minerals—Juvenile literature. I. Title. II. Series.
  QE365.2.S76 2004
  549—dc22                                         2004023085

About the Author

Darlene R. Stille is a science writer and author of more than 70 books for young people. When she was in high school, she fell in love with science. While attending the University of Illinois, she discovered that she also loved writing. She was fortunate enough to find a career as an editor and writer that allowed her to combine both of her interests. Darlene Stille now lives and writes in Michigan.

*c h a p t e r*                                              *p a g e*

**1**   WHAT IS A MINERAL?.................................................................**4**

**2**   THE ELEMENTS OF MINERALS.......................................**10**

**3**   PROPERTIES OF MINERALS............................................**18**

**4**   MINERALS FOUND IN ROCKS.......................................**30**

**5**   ORE MINERALS.....................................................................**36**


*Glossary* ..........................................................*45*

*Did You Know?* .................................................*46*

*Further Resources* ............................................*47*

*Index* ..............................................................*48*

# CHAPTER ONE

# What Is a Mineral?

Does a sphalerite sound like an alien from another planet? Does cinnabar sound like something you buy at a bakery? Mica is not a person's name, and fluorite is not something added to toothpaste to stop tooth decay. These are the names of minerals.

The mineral fluorite exists in many colors, including red, yellow, green, and purple.

A mineral is natural, solid material that is not alive. About 3,000 kinds of minerals are the building blocks of all rocks on Earth. In a slab of colorful granite, each different speckle is a mineral. Even in a smooth, black rock there are microscopic pieces of different minerals all mixed together.

Most particles in soil are minerals, too, as are metals, such as copper and silver. Many fossils are minerals that took on the shape of animals that lived millions of years ago.

Some minerals are easy to find. Ordinary table salt is a common mineral. The "lead" in pencils is actually made of the mineral graphite. The walls in your house or apartment are most likely

Individual specks of the minerals quartz and feldspar can be seen in a slab of granite.

## Mineral Wars

Throughout history, the quest for minerals has caused conflicts and wars. The ancient Romans, for example, tried to defeat the Celts in southern England to take control of their tin mines.

Gold has been the cause of many conflicts, large and small. Spain conquered much of Central and South America in the 1500s in an attempt to find Native American gold. Pirates raided Spanish ships hauling the gold back to Spain.

Sierra Leone is a major diamond producer. During the 1990s, diamonds were the cause of much suffering in this African country. Rival groups fought for control of the country and financed their war with smuggled diamonds, which came to be called "blood diamonds."

In this historical painting, Hernan Cortes (left), a Spanish explorer, poses next to Montezuma, an Aztec Indian who ruled what is now Mexico in the early 1500s.

made of drywall, which is made from the mineral gypsum. Other minerals such as diamond and gold are very rare, which is why they cost so much in jewelry.

## A STRICT DEFINITION

Mineralogists, scientists who study minerals, strictly define what a mineral is. A mineral is only found in nature. Nothing made in a laboratory or factory is a mineral. Synthetic diamonds and other manufactured gemstones are not true minerals.

Scientists call minerals inorganic material, which, except for a few instances, means they were never alive. Material from animals or plants is called organic material. People sometimes call coal, oil, and other fossil fuels "mineral resources" because they come out of the earth. Fossil fuels, however, are not minerals because they formed from organic material—plants and animals that died millions of years ago.

On a food label, you may have seen lists of vitamins and so-called minerals contained in that food. However, such food minerals as iron, calcium, sodium, and zinc are not considered true minerals by mineralogists.

Huge piles of salt are mined from underground deposits. The deposits formed when salty seawater evaporated from ancient oceans millions of years ago.

The general chemical makeup of a mineral is always the same no matter where it is found. A diamond found in Asia has the same chemical makeup as a diamond found in Africa. Sand is a mixture of minerals, but is not a mineral by itself. Sand on a beach in Hawaii has a different chemical makeup from sand on a beach in the Caribbean Sea.

A mineral is always a solid. It can never be a liquid or a gas. Like all matter, minerals are made up of microscopic atoms. The difference between minerals and other solids has to do with how the atoms are arranged inside the mineral. Atoms in minerals are neatly organized into crystals.

## WHAT IS A MINERAL CRYSTAL?

A crystal is a three-dimensional structure. Salt crystals, for example, are cubes. Other crystals can be pyramids or hundreds of other shapes.

Like all minerals, a natural diamond's chemical makeup is generally consistent no matter where it comes from. Today, the world's major diamond mines are in the African nations of Botswana, Namibia, and South Africa.

## SALT CRYSTALS

Cubes of sodium and chlorine atoms stack on top of each ·········▶ other and side by side to form salt crystals.

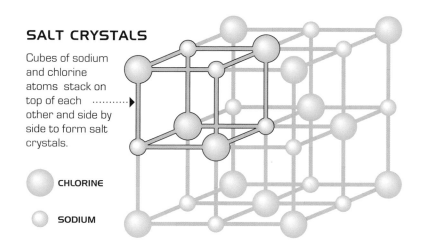

◯ CHLORINE

◯ SODIUM

Atoms in a crystal are organized into a pattern that repeats itself over and over again. This basic pattern of a crystal's atoms is called a unit cell. A unit cell is like an apartment in a building where each apartment is exactly the same. The apartments are stacked on top of each other and side-by-side to create a structure. In a similar manner, unit cells grow on top of and around each other to create mineral crystals.

**FAST FACT:** One of the softest minerals, graphite, and one of the hardest minerals, diamond, are both made of only carbon atoms. Their differences result from the structures of their crystals.

# The Elements of Minerals

**AN ELEMENT** is a substance made up of only one kind of atom. For example, gold has only gold atoms, while a compound, such as salt, is made up of sodium and chlorine atoms. There are 91 natural chemical elements, and they come together in thousands of combinations to make up all matter on Earth, including minerals. However, elements do not exist in equal amounts. In fact, only eight elements make up almost all of the minerals in Earth's rocky outer layer, or crust.

### ELEMENTS IN EARTH'S CRUST

Oxygen accounts for nearly half the weight of Earth's crust. This may be surprising, since we most often think of oxygen as the gas we breathe. Oxygen atoms, however, combine with atoms from other elements to create many kinds of minerals.

### Percent of Earth's Crust by Weight

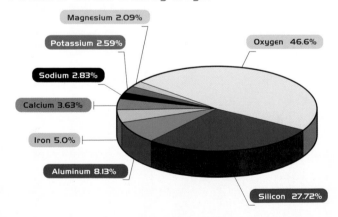

Magnesium 2.09%

Potassium 2.59%

Sodium 2.83%

Calcium 3.63%

Iron 5.0%

Aluminum 8.13%

Oxygen 46.6%

Silicon 27.72%

## WHERE DID THE ELEMENTS COME FROM?

Most scientists believe that the first elements formed about 15 billion years ago, soon after the universe began with an explosion called the Big Bang. At first, there were just two elements, hydrogen and helium. The first stars formed from giant clouds of hydrogen and helium gas. The swirling clouds were pulled together by the force of their own gravity. The smaller they got, the faster they swirled until they became a ball of gas. The inside of the ball grew hotter. The matter grew denser, or more tightly packed.

When the matter was hot and dense enough, nuclear fusion reactions began inside the star's atoms. Nuclear fusion reactions

New stars form inside a giant dust cloud.

push the centers, or nuclei, of two atoms so closely together that they join, or fuse. This gives off huge amounts of energy that makes the star shine.

The fusion reactions that make stars shine also created new chemical elements. Nuclear fusion changed hydrogen and helium atoms into atoms of new elements, such as nitrogen and oxygen. Then nuclear fusion changed nitrogen and oxygen into other new elements. Those new elements were further changed until all 91 elements, from hydrogen to sulfur to lead, came to be.

## HOW NUCLEAR FUSION WORKS

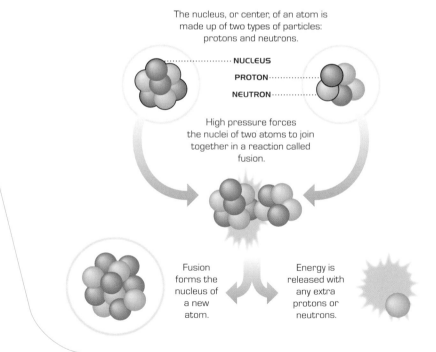

The nucleus, or center, of an atom is made up of two types of particles: protons and neutrons.

NUCLEUS

PROTON

NEUTRON

High pressure forces the nuclei of two atoms to join together in a reaction called fusion.

Fusion forms the nucleus of a new atom.

Energy is released with any extra protons or neutrons.

## HOW DID THE ELEMENTS GET TO EARTH?

As a star grows older, it begins to run out of atoms for nuclear fusion. A very large star has a spectacular death. It ends with a huge explosion called a supernova. The explosion blows off clouds of gas and dust into space. The clouds drift in outer space until gravity starts pulling the gas and dust together to form a new star.

Geologists and other planetary scientists believe that Earth, our sun, moon, and solar system formed billions of years ago from just such a swirling cloud of gas and dust. The cloud contained all the chemical elements formed in an ancient star. As part of the cloud condensed to form a planet, the chemical elements came together to form minerals. The minerals came together to form the first rocks on Earth.

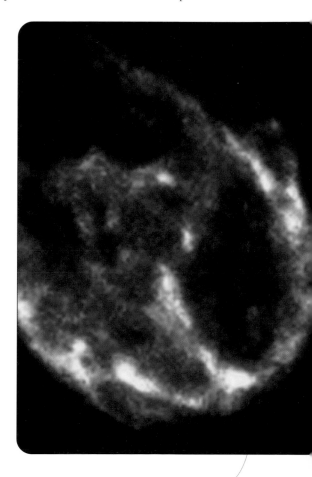

A giant cloud of dust hurls through space after a supernova. At 80 light-years across, it is trillions of times larger than Earth.

# HOW PLANETS FORMED IN THE UNIVERSE

### I Big Bang

Scientists believe that matter began to form about 15 billion years ago after an enormous explosion, known as the Big Bang. Clouds of hydrogen and helium then began to form.

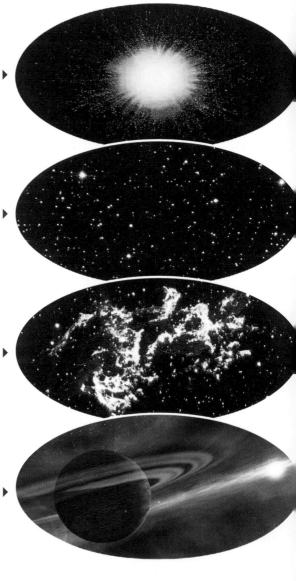

### 2 First Stars

The gas clouds were forced together by gravity to create dense balls. High temperature inside these gas balls caused atoms to fuse together and form new elements. Energy released from these fusions ignited the first stars.

### 3 Supernova

Stars continued to produce energy and shine until they ran out of atoms for nuclear fusion. Larger stars exploded in an event called a supernova, and they scattered clouds of gas and dust into space.

### 4 New Planets

Gravity pulled the gas and dust together to form Earth and other planets.

Images courtesy of NASA

## Moon Minerals

On July 20, 1969, the first astronauts landed on the moon. One of the major goals of the *Apollo* moon mission was to collect rocks and bring them back to Earth. Scientists believed that moon rocks had an important story to tell. They were right.

The rocks the astronauts collected turned out to be basalt and breccias. Geologists knew that basalt on Earth is hardened lava that comes from volcanoes. Lava coming out of volcanoes is sometimes so hot that it runs like a river of fire. After studying the moon's basalt, geologists concluded that at one time, the moon must have been a really hot place with parts covered by flowing lava.

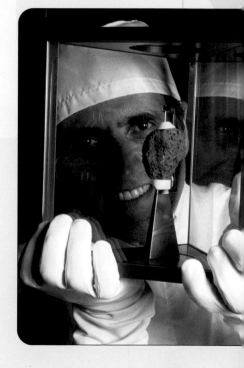

Scientists also knew that craters on the moon's surface were caused by meteoroids and comets that had repeatedly crashed into the moon. The breccias were further evidence that this was the case. Breccias are sedimentary rocks made of rock pieces pressed together. The force of big objects from space plummeting down on the moon would be powerful enough to form breccias.

A geologist holds a piece of basalt found during one of the *Apollo* moon missions.

## MINERAL CLASSES

Mineralogists have identified about 3,000 different minerals on Earth. They keep track of all these minerals by classifying them, just as biologists classify animals and plants. First, mineralogists group minerals into eight major classes according to the elements they contain and how the atoms are combined. The largest class of minerals is the silicates, which account for about 95 percent of the rocks in Earth's crust.

Mineralogists divide these eight major classes into more specific and smaller categories based on chemical makeup and structure. Classes are first divided into families, which are further divided into groups. In turn, groups are made up of species, the most specific classification.

Gold/Native element

Barite/Sulfate

# MAJOR MINERAL CLASSES

| Class | Chemical feature | Minerals in this class |
|---|---|---|
| Native elements | All atoms are the same kind | gold, diamond, iron |
| Sulfides | Contain a form of sulfur | pyrite, galena, sphalerite |
| Halides | Contain sodium and chlorine | halite (salt), fluorite |
| Carbonates | Contain carbon | calcite, aragonite, dolomite |
| Sulfates | Contain a form of sulfur | gypsum, barite, anhydrite |
| Oxides | Contain oxygen with a metal | hematite, chromite, rulite |
| Phosphates | Contain phosphorous | apatite |
| Silicates | Contain silicon and oxygen | quartz, feldspar, olivine |

Pyrite/Sulfide

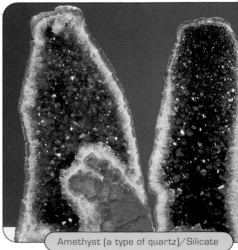

Amethyst (a type of quartz)/Silicate

# CHAPTER THREE

# Properties of Minerals

**WITH ALL** the thousands of minerals around, how can you tell one mineral from another? Mineralogists have developed ways of identifying minerals according to a set of qualities, or properties.

Mineral properties serve many useful functions. Geologists use mineral properties to identify rocks and valuable ores, and jewelers use them to identify and price gemstones. An engineer's plans for a building could rely on the properties of minerals in the stone that is being used. Mineral properties help rock collectors figure out what kinds of stones and minerals they have found.

Some of the main properties used to identify minerals are color, streak, luster, hardness, and cleavage.

### COLOR

Minerals come in a rainbow array of spectacular colors, from stark white to pitch black to deep red. Often, a mineral's color is due to the elements that make up its crystals. Bright red cinnabar gets its color from red mercuric sulfide, a chemical compound of the elements mercury and sulfur. Other minerals get their color from chemical impurities, or substances that are not ordinarily part of the mineral's crystals. For example, quartz is a clear, colorless mineral in its pure state. In nature, however, quartz is found in several colors. Quartz with a bluish-violet color is called amethyst. This color

comes from iron and manganese impurities. Other impurities can turn quartz green, pink, or black. Because of impurities, color is not always a reliable way to identify minerals.

## STREAK

Rock collectors often use streak to identify a mineral. Streak is the color of the powder a mineral leaves when it is rubbed across

Deep red cinnabar's color is caused by its chemical makeup. The clear crystals are pure quartz.

a rough surface. Rock collectors rub minerals on a streak plate made of unglazed porcelain.

Because the streak a mineral leaves is not always the color of the mineral, streak can help tell the difference between two minerals that are the same color. A lump of pyrite is a worthless iron mineral that, on the surface, looks like gold. Gold prospectors in the 1800s used to tell the difference between real gold and pyrite, or "fool's gold," by their streaks. Real gold has a gold streak. Gold-colored pyrite has a black streak.

Like many minerals, hematite can leave a streak that is a different color from its general color. Here, a chunk of grey hematite leaves a brown streak.

## LUSTER

Luster is a property that describes how rays of light are reflected off the surface of a mineral. Minerals have two main types of luster, called metallic and nonmetallic.

Metallic luster is shiny. Gold has a very shiny metallic luster. Minerals with a nonmetallic luster have different looks, including pearly, glassy, silky, or dull. Talc has a pearly surface. Quartz has a glassy surface. The luster of graphite is dull. Cinnabar can have either a metallic or a dull, nonmetallic luster.

Quartz has a glassy, nonmetallic luster, while galena and pyrite have a shiny, metallic luster.

## HARDNESS

A mineral's hardness describes how easily the mineral can be scratched. A German mineralogist named Friedrich Mohs in 1822 invented a scale for measuring hardness. He picked 10 minerals representing the softest to the hardest and gave each one a number from 1 to 10. Softer minerals have low numbers, and harder minerals have high numbers.

On his scale, the hardness of a mineral depends on whether it can scratch another mineral. For example, apatite (5) can scratch fluorite (4), but fluorite cannot scratch apatite. Many minerals fall between two numbers on the scale. For example, galena can scratch gypsum (2) but not calcite (3). So the hardness of galena is between gypsum and calcite, or 2.5.

At 10, the hardest mineral is diamond. Diamond can scratch any other kind of mineral, but nothing can scratch a diamond except another diamond.

**FAST FACT:** Even though diamond is the hardest mineral, a diamond can be destroyed by heat. If a diamond is heated along with oxygen, it will burn and give off carbon dioxide gas. If it is heated in a box that contains no oxygen, the diamond will turn into graphite, one of the softest minerals.

## MOHS HARDNESS SCALE

**A hardness of 5 is just a little bit softer than glass.**
**A hardness of 2.5 is about the same as a fingernail.**

1. Talc
2. Gypsum
3. Calcite
4. Fluorite
5. Apatite
6. Orthoclase feldspar
7. Quartz
8. Topaz
9. Corundum
10. Diamond

Talc (1)

Apatite (5)

## Friedrich Mohs, Rock Scratcher

Friedrich Mohs became interested in scratching minerals while he was studying the rock collection of a wealthy Austrian banker. Mohs was born in Germany in 1773 and was educated in math, physics, and chemistry. A teacher got him interested in minerals, and in 1802, Mohs moved to Vienna, Austria, to organize the banker's mineral collection.

At that time, most mineralogists classified minerals according the their chemical makeup. Mohs thought they should be classified according to physical properties—how they looked and felt. He began studying hardness by scratching one mineral with another. In 1822, Mohs invented his famous scale. Today, mineralogists still rely on the Mohs Hardness Scale to determine a mineral's hardness.

## CLEAVAGE

Cleavage is a property of minerals that refers to the way they split apart when hit. A mineral with good cleavage will split along weak points in its structure. It breaks into pieces with flat surfaces, or planes. Minerals with poor cleavage, such as quartz, break into jagged pieces or splinter into fibers the way asbestos does.

Minerals can cleave, or split, in different numbers of directions. The pieces' flat surfaces may meet at different angles, too. Mica cleaves in one direction to form thin sheets, like a deck of

Asbestos has poor cleavage. It splinters into fibers.

cards. A diamond cleaves in four directions to form a pyramid shape. Other minerals with good cleavage can split in up to six directions.

## OTHER WAYS TO IDENTIFY MINERALS

Sometimes rock collectors simply feel a mineral sample. Talc, for example, feels greasy. It is also the softest mineral, with a hardness of 1.

Crystal habit refers to the general shape of a mineral. Quartz is usually in the form of long, thin crystals, while diamond crystals are blocky.

Specific gravity is a ratio that shows how much a mineral weighs compared with an equal volume of water. Diamond has a specific gravity of 3.52, which means a diamond weighs about $3^{1}/_{2}$ times more than an equal volume of water.

There are many chemical tests for identifying minerals. For example, you can pour a weak acid, such as vinegar or lemon

Mica cleaves into thin sheets. This is because the atoms in mica are also arranged in thin sheets.

juice, on a mineral. If the mineral is in the carbonates class, the acid will fizz. Acid will react with the mineral to create carbon dioxide gas. The gas bubbles are what make the fizz.

**FAST FACT:** Some minerals glow. Minerals such as scheelite have a property called fluorescence. Rock collectors use ultraviolet light to find these minerals at night. Shining invisible ultraviolet rays on the minerals makes them give off visible light.

Acid causes bubbles to form on a block of calcite, a mineral in the carbonates class.

## Gems and Jewels

A diamond ring glitters on the finger of a bride. Emeralds, rubies, and sapphires sparkle in the showcase of a jewelry store. Precious gemstones have long been prized for their beauty and value.

What makes a mineral a gemstone? Gemstones are minerals with extraordinary color, sparkle, and hardness.

Color is a major factor in determining the value of a gem. The best and most expensive diamonds, for example, are clear. Most diamonds have a yellow tint. Others are black, blue, brown, green, pink, and purple. The colors are caused by impurities.

A property called the index of refraction measures a gem's sparkle. It tells how much a ray of light bends as it passes through a transparent gemstone. Light slows down when it passes from air through another material. The slowing causes the light rays to bend. The more the rays bend, the more brilliant the material looks. The extreme bending of light makes diamonds flash and sparkle.

A mineral has to be hard in order to be used in jewelry. Gems have to be rated at least 7 on the Mohs Hardness Scale. Diamonds are rated 10. Only diamond can cut diamond. Professionals called lapidaries use metal wheels coated with diamond dust to cut and polish diamonds.

The final beauty of a gem comes from its cut. Lapidaries cut gems into one of two main styles—faceted or cabochon. A faceted cut has many smooth sides. The cabochon style is rounded. Transparent gems, such as diamonds and sapphires, have faceted cuts. Opaque (nontransparent) gems, such as agate and turquoise, have cabochon cuts. Then the gem is set in gold, silver, or platinum to become a valued ring, necklace, or brooch.

A lapidary examines a diamond through a magnifying glass.

# CHAPTER FOUR

## ⊕ Minerals Found in Rocks

OF ALL EARTH'S 3,000 minerals, only about 100 are commonly found in rocks. Most others are more rare than gold. However, these 100 common minerals are not equally abundant. For example, feldspars alone make up about 60 percent of Earth's crust. Other important minerals in rocks are quartz and calcite. These minerals all have unique properties and uses.

### FELDSPAR

Feldspar is the name of a group of minerals in the silicates class. Feldspars are hard, ranking 6 on the Mohs Hardness Scale. They come in different colors, such as blue, gray, green, pink, or white.

Feldspars have many uses. Nature uses weathering to break down feldspars to form clay, an important part of soil. In industry, some clay can be made into coating for paper. A type of white clay call kaolin is used to make fine china.

Along with quartz, feldspars make up a rock called granite. Granite is an important building material. Polished granite is popular for kitchen countertops.

Feldspars such as this one are one of Earth's most abundant minerals.

Some feldspars are beautiful enough to be gemstones. Moonstone, for example, is a whitish feldspar. It is the birthstone of people born in June.

Granite is cut away at Rock of Ages, Vermont, the world's largest granite quarry.

### QUARTZ

Quartz, a mineral in the silicates class, is the most common mineral in Earth's crust after feldspar. It is the mineral most often found in sand and in a type of rock called sandstone.

At 7 on the Mohs Hardness Scale, quartz is a hard mineral. It takes longer for weathering and erosion to wear away quartz than other kinds of common minerals in rock.

Electric current can pass through quartz crystals and make them expand or contract. This property makes quartz valuable for making all kinds of electronic products. Quartz is used in radio and television tuners and in battery-operated watches.

Quartz is a common, versatile mineral with many uses in nature and industry.

A type of quartz called rock crystal is so clear that it is used to make lenses for microscopes and telescopes. Quartz is heat resistant, so it is also used to make glass baking pans and dishes.

## CALCITE

Calcite is a soft mineral in the carbonates class. It is 3 on the Mohs Hardness Scale. Some calcite can be found in most types of rocks. Calcite is the chief mineral in limestone and chalk, a soft, white form of limestone. Calcite is also the chief mineral in marble.

Calcite can take many forms and have a variety of uses. Calcite in limestone is important for making cement and mortar. Marble is used for tile on walls and floors. Sculptors use marble to carve statues. Mexican onyx is a type of calcite that can be carved into animals and other figurines. This heavy form of calcite also makes good bookends.

Limestone, which is almost completely made of calcite, is usually white but may have colored streaks as it does here. The streaks are caused by impurities.

## Cave Minerals

Rocks shaped like icicles hang down from the ceiling of a cave. Columns of rock rise up from the cave floor. The "icicles" are called stalactites, and the columns are called stalagmites. Stalactites and stalagmites are made of the mineral calcite.

Stalactites and stalagmites form over thousands of years as underground water drips from the ceiling and walls of a limestone cave. Water dripping from the cave ceiling dissolves calcite from the rock. The water evaporates, leaving the calcite to build up bit by bit into long, skinny stalagmites. Calcite from water drops that reach the floor builds up columns of stalagmites. You can see awesome stalactites and stalagmites in the Carlsbad Caverns of New Mexico and Mammoth Cave in Kentucky.

Stalactites (top) and stalagmites (bottom) at Carlsbad Caverns, New Mexico

## OTHER IMPORTANT MINERALS IN ROCK

Olivine is a hard mineral, between 6.5 and 7 on the Mohs Hardness Scale. Olivine can be green, yellow-green, or brown. Clear green olivine is a precious stone called peridot used in jewelry.

Minerals in the pyroxene group are abundant not only in Earth's crust, but they are also in rocks found on the moon. Pyroxenes can be colorless or different colors from dark green to reddish brown. Their crystals are shaped like pyramids with four sides. The hardness of pyroxene minerals ranges from 5 to 7 on the Mohs Hardness Scale.

Garnet is a group of minerals that are hard and have a glassy luster. Garnets can be many colors—brown, black, red, yellow, or green. Some garnets are used as inexpensive gemstones. Because this mineral is so hard, it is used for grinding and polishing other materials.

Peridot, a form of olivine that is used in jewelry, is the birthstone of people born in August.

# CHAPTER FIVE

# Ore Minerals

**ORE MINERALS** are minerals that hold enough metal to make them worthwhile for mining. The concentration of metal in an ore is what determines its value. The amount varies from mineral to mineral.

For example, because iron is cheap, businesses won't bother mining iron ore that has less than 50 percent metal in it. Because it takes a lot of energy to extract aluminum from ore, companies generally only mine aluminum ore that has at least 30 percent metal in it. Expensive metals such as silver or platinum, however, will be extracted from ores with 0.01 percent metal or less.

Ores lie among other kinds of rock. Thin deposits of ore are called veins. Large ore deposits are called beds. Ores come from

A bright blue vein of molybdenite runs through rock. Molybdenite is the main ore of the metal molybdenum, which is used to strengthen steel.

one of two kinds of mines. In open pit mines, earthmoving machinery first scrapes away the top layers of soil and rock. Then explosives are used to break up the ore, and power shovels scoop out the pieces. In shaft mines, miners dig tunnels underground to reach the ore deposits.

Most ores are compound ores. Metals in compound ores are chemically combined with some other element, such as oxygen or sulfur. When metals combine with oxygen, the mineral is called an oxide. Sulfides are minerals in which the metal is joined with sulfur.

Iron ore turns the water bright orange at an open pit mine in Brazil.

## CHIEF COMPOUND ORES

| Name | Metal | Type | Uses |
|---|---|---|---|
| Bauxite | Aluminum | Oxide | Beverage cans, aluminum foil, airplane bodies |
| Cassiterite | Tin | Oxide | Coating on steel cans used for packaging food |
| Chalcopyrite | Copper | Sulfide | Making brass; electrical wiring, pipes, locks |
| Cinnabar | Mercury | Sulfide | Electric switches, fluorescent lamps |
| Galena | Lead | Sulfide | Batteries, machine parts |
| Hematite | Iron | Oxide | Making steel; machine parts, fences, chains |
| Pentlandite | Nickel | Sulfide | Making steel; industrial processes |
| Sphalerite | Zinc | Sulfide | Making brass; rustproof coating on other metals |

Sphalerite/Zinc ore

Chalcopyrite/Copper ore

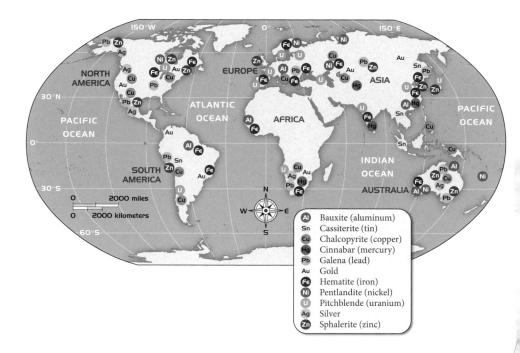

| | |
|---|---|
| Al | Bauxite (aluminum) |
| Sn | Cassiterite (tin) |
| Cu | Chalcopyrite (copper) |
| Hg | Cinnabar (mercury) |
| Pb | Galena (lead) |
| Au | Gold |
| Fe | Hematite (iron) |
| Ni | Pentlandite (nickel) |
| U | Pitchblende (uranium) |
| Ag | Silver |
| Zn | Sphalerite (zinc) |

Some ores, called native metals, hold chunks of pure metal. Gold, for example, can be in the form of pure gold nuggets or in veins. Other native metals can be copper, platinum, and silver.

**FAST FACT:** Canada, Russia, and the United States are nations rich in mineral resources, including iron, gold, salt, silver, and zinc. China produces the most tin. Russia has the most nickel. Australia is the world's leading aluminum producer.

This map shows major ore deposits around the world.

## California Gold Rush

One January day in 1848, a carpenter named James Marshall was working on the American River in California, building a sawmill for John Sutter. He saw something the size of a pea gleaming in the river. Gold! All day, Marshall and his crew of builders kept finding gold nuggets. Marshall and Sutter tried to keep the discovery a secret, but word got out, and the great California Gold Rush was on.

Gold throughout history has been a powerful force, drawing people to far-off places. It drew people by the thousands to California. The first shipload of prospectors arrived in San Francisco in February 1849. The year before, only 15,000 people lived in this remote area. By the end of 1849, the population swelled to more than 100,000.

The prospectors, nicknamed the Forty-Niners, panned for gold in rivers and streams. They sifted through sand and gravel, looking for the gleaming nuggets. The deposits of gold they mined were called placer deposits, one of two main kinds of gold deposits. Placer deposits contain little gold nuggets that accumulate in sand and gravel. Most gold is in lode deposits, which are veins of gold locked up in solid rock. It's hard work mining gold out of rock. Gold in placer deposits is just there for the taking.

The prospectors found plenty of gold in California. The problem was, with so many prospectors, everything else—from tools to food—was in short supply. Prices skyrocketed. One egg cost 50 cents. Flour was a dollar a pint.

The people who got rich from the Gold Rush were the merchants who supplied the Forty-Niners. Soon the gold ran out, and many prospectors went broke and turned to other occupations. One side effect of the Gold Rush was that it gave California enough people to become a state in 1850.

Starting in 1849, prospectors called the Forty-Niners flocked to California in search of gold. Most traveled west over land in covered wagons and on foot.

## ORES AND THE ENVIRONMENT

Most ores come from open pit mines. Some of these mines have damaged the environment, leaving huge scars on the land. Wastes from ore mining, called tailings, can pollute nearby water. Tailings from iron ore were once dumped into, and polluted, Lake Superior. In 1978, the United States and Canada signed an agreement to clean up and protect the waters of Lake Superior. Today, it is one of the least polluted of the Great Lakes.

Ores are being used at increasing rates. Deposits of copper, lead, nickel, and zinc ores may run out within 100 years. Meanwhile, mining companies first dig up ores with the highest metal

content, called high-grade ores. As high-grade ores run out, the companies turn to lower-grade ores. These ores use much more energy to refine.

## BAUXITE AND ALUMINUM CANS

Bauxite is an example of an ore that requires huge amounts of energy to process. Aluminum refined from bauxite is used to make many kinds of products, from airplane bodies to aluminum foil and aluminum cans.

Aluminum ore, or bauxite, is difficult and expensive to refine.

There is no immediate danger that the world will run out of bauxite. There is enough bauxite remaining to last hundreds of years. The problem with bauxite is that it takes a tremendous amount of electric energy to refine it into aluminum. Producing so much energy uses up coal, oil, and other fossil fuels. Burning the fossil fuels to make energy causes air pollution.

Machines scrape away soil to uncover bauxite at an open pit mine in Jamaica.

The answer to the bauxite problem lies in recycling. Soda and other beverage cans are an important part of the recycling effort. Refining bauxite takes so much electrical energy that recycling just one soda can saves enough energy to light a 100-watt bulb for more than three hours. About one-third of the aluminum products made in the United States come from the recycled metal.

Conserving mineral resources is a major problem. Often, there is no good substitute for a metal made from ore. The best hope of being sure the world does not run out of these natural resources seems to be finding more and better ways of recycling existing products.

Recycling beverage cans is one of the best ways to reduce bauxite use and conserve energy. Manufacturing a soda can from scratch takes four times as much energy as it does to recycle one.

**Big Bang**—the enormous explosion that created the universe about 15 billion years ago, according to one widely believed scientific theory

**fluorescence**—a property of minerals that makes them give off visible light when certain forms of energy, such as ultraviolet light, are applied to them

**fossil**—the remains of an ancient plant or animal that have hardened into rock; also the preserved tracks or outline of an ancient organism

**geologists**—scientists who study how Earth formed and how it changes by examining soil, rocks, rivers, and other landforms

**meteoroids**—rocky or metallic chunks of matter traveling through space

**mortar**—a cementlike mixture used in construction that, once hardened, binds together bricks and stones

**nuclei**—the centers of atoms that are made up of protons and neutrons; *nuclei* is the plural of *nucelus*

**prospector**—a person who looks for valuable minerals, especially silver and gold

**ratio**—a comparison of two quantities expressed in numbers; for example, the ratio of the sun to planets in our solar system is 1 to 9

**sedimentary rock**—rock formed by layers of sediment, such as sand and mud, being pressed together

**supernova**—explosion of a very large star at the end of its life that gives off tremendous amounts of energy

**synthetic**—artificial or manufactured

**ultraviolet light**—rays of light that cannot be seen by the human eye

**weathering**—the breaking up of rocks and soil, mainly by wind and water

▸ The mineral magnetite has an unusual property—magnetism. The black rock called lodestone is made of magnetite. An ancient Greek legend tells that a shepherd discovered this natural magnet when the iron nails in his boots stuck to a rock. Early sailors used lodestone to make compasses. A sliver of lodestone suspended by a string always pointed north and south.

▸ Prehistoric people found pure iron in meteorites that had landed on Earth from outer space. They heated the metal in fire and shaped it into tools. Around 4,000 B.C., ancient people learned how to remove iron from ores, leading to a period of history called the Iron Age, when most tools were made of this metal.

▸ The oldest minerals dated on Earth are crystals of the mineral zircon. Scientists announced in 2001 that they had found zircon crystals that are 4.4 billion years old. The crystals survived so long because zircon is a very hard mineral that is difficult to scratch. Therefore, it was able to withstand the forces of weathering and erosion.

▸ Muscovite, which is not very hard, is a mineral that cleaves into thin, flexible sheets. Bend them, and they will go back to their original shape. Muscovite can be either clear or tinted yellow, green, or brown. Muscovite was once used as window glass by Russians, who were also called Muscovites, after their capital Moscow.

▸ When pyrite, or "fool's gold," is struck with a hammer, sparks are produced. In the past, some American Indians and members of a number of other cultures used pyrite to make fire.

▸ Rocks and minerals were some of the earliest raw materials used by people. Prehistoric people made knives and axes out of stone during a period called the Stone Age. They carved flint, a rock made of microscopic quartz crystals, into sharp arrowheads and spearheads.

Prehistoric people carved flint arrowheads and spearheads such as these.

## At the Library

Graham, Ian. *Minerals: A Resource Our World Depends On.* Chicago:
Heinemann Library, 2005.
Ricciuti, Edward R., and Margaret W. Carruthers. *National Audubon Society
First Field Guide to Rocks and Minerals.* New York: Scholastic, 1998.
Schumann, Walter. *Gemstones of the World.* New York: Sterling, 2004
Symes, R. F. *Rocks & Minerals.* New York: DK Publishing, 2004.

## On the Web

For more information on **minerals,** use FactHound to track down Web sites
related to this book.
   1. Go to *www.facthound.com*
   2. Type in a search word related to this
      book or this book ID: **075650855X.**
   3. Click on the *Fetch It* button.
FactHound will find the best Web sites for you.

## On the Road

**Crater of Diamonds State Park**
   209 State Park Road
   Murfreesboro, AR 71958
   870/285-3113
   *www.arkansasstateparks.com*
   To find real diamonds and other gemstones at this Arkansas state park

**A. E. Seaman Mineral Museum**
   Michigan Technological University
   1400 Townsend Drive
   Houghton, MI 49931-1295
   906/487-2572
   *www.museum.mtu.edu*
   To see a collection of more than 20,000 minerals

**Weinman Mineral Museum**
   51 Mineral Museum Drive
   White, Georgia 30184
   770/386-0576
   *www.weinmanmuseum.org*
   To tour exhibits about all kinds of minerals, from fossils to cave
   formations

agate, 29
aluminum, 10, 36, 38, 42–44
apatite, 17, 22, 23
atoms, 8–9, 17

basalt, 15
bauxite, 38, 42–44
Big Bang, 11, 14
breccias, 15

cabochon cut, 29
calcite, 22, 23, 33–34
California gold rush, 40–41
carbonates, 17, 33–34
cave minerals, 34
Celts, ancient, 6
chemical makeup, 8
cinnabar, 18, 19, 21, 38
classes of minerals, 16–17
clay, 30
cleavage, 24–26
color, 18–19, 28, 30, 35
compounds, 10, 37–38
conservation, 44
crystal habit, 26
crystals, 8–9, 35

description, 5, 7–8
diamonds
    chemical feature of, 17
    cleavage of, 26
    color of, 28
    conflicts about, 6
    crystal habit of, 9, 26
    cut of, 29
    hardness of, 22, 23, 28
    specific gravity of, 26
    value of, 7

Earth, crust of, 10, 16, 30, 32
elements, 10, 11–12, 18
energy, 42–44
environmental damage, 42, 43

faceted cut, 28–29
families of minerals, 16
feel, 26
feldspars, 30–31
fluorescence, 27
food minerals, 7
fool's gold, 20
Forty-Niners, 40

fossil fuels, 7
fossils, 5

galena, 22, 38
garnets, 35
gemstones, 28–29, 31, 35. See also diamonds
gold
    California gold rush, 40–41
    conflicts about, 6
    deposits, 39, 40
    luster of, 21
    streak of, 20
    value of, 7
granite, 30
graphite, 5, 9, 21, 22
groups of minerals, 16
gypsum, 7, 22, 23

hardness, 22–24, 30, 32, 33, 35
helium, 11, 14
hydrogen, 11, 14

identification, 26–27. See also properties
index of refraction, 28
inorganic materials, described, 7
iron, 36, 42

Lake Superior, 42
limestone, 33
luster, 21

marble, 33
Marshall, James, 40
metals, 5, 36
Mexican onyx, 33
mica, 25–26
mining, 36–37, 42
Mohs Hardness Scale, 22, 23, 24, 28
moon minerals, 15, 35
moonstones, 31

native metals, 39
nitrogen, 12
nuclear fusion, 11–12, 13, 14

olivine, 35
ore deposits, 36–37, 40

organic materials, described, 7
oxygen, 10, 12, 17, 22, 37

planets formed, 11, 13, 14
pollution, 42, 43
properties
    cleavage, 24–26
    color, 18–19, 28, 30, 35
    crystal habit, 26
    feel, 26
    fluorescence, 27
    hardness, 22–24
    index of refraction, 28
    luster, 21
    specific gravity, 26
    streak, 19–20
pyrite, 20
pyroxenes, 35

quartz, 32–34
    cleavage of, 24
    color of, 18–19
    crystal habit of, 26
    in granite, 30
    hardness of, 23
    luster of, 21

recycling, 44
refining, 42–44
rocks, 5, 13, 30–36
Romans, ancient, 6

salt, 5, 8–9
sapphires, 29
scheelite, 27
silicates, 16, 17, 30–33
species of minerals, 16
specific gravity, 26
stalactites, 34
stalagmites, 34
streak, 19–20
sulfur, 17, 37
supernova, 13, 14
Sutter, John, 40

tailings, 42
talc, 21, 23, 26
turquoise, 29

unit cells, 9

zinc, 38, 39